London
Undercurrents

The hidden histories
of London's unsung heroines,
north and south of the river

by Joolz Sparkes and Hilaire

Holland Park Press London

Published by Holland Park Press 2019

First Edition

A CIP catalogue record for this book is
available from The British Library.

ISBN 978-1-907320-82-8

Cover designed by Reactive Graphics

Printed and bound by
CPI Group (UK) Ltd, Croydon CR0 4YY

www.hollandparkpress.co.uk

London Undercurrents is a collaboration by two London-based female poets Joolz Sparkes (N) and Hilaire (S). This poetry cycle gives a voice to women who often go unheard.

There are thousands of women, extraordinary, ordinary, famous or forgotten who have plenty to say and deserve to be heard. The authors want to share the hidden histories of London's unsung heroines that they have uncovered in their neighbourhoods north (N) and south (S) of the river.

London Undercurrents shows that the personal is also universal and casts women as the central characters of their own story.

This collection is one of a kind, fascinating and well researched. It really captures the spirit, image and diversity of London.

CONTENTS

PAVED
WITH
GOLD

I search for my home on the map;
the road isn't built yet.

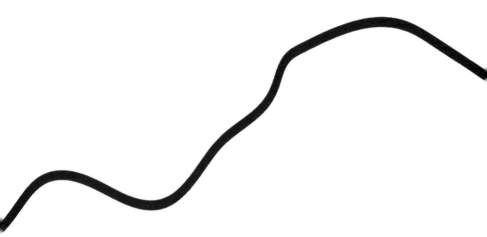

Battersea crept up on me.
The soil got under my fingernails
into my lungs.

FIRST CROP
A Huguenot Woman in Battersea Fields, 1685

We did not say a word
that bitter February morning.
Just let our hands probe
the river-rich soil,
let a seed grow between us:
the idea of green tips.
Asperge.
The Thames
funnelled a gale inland,
the salt-cut air smelt good.
I trusted
my husband's feel
for *terroir.*
He banked on
my bounteous patience,
my *savoir-faire.*
Signed his name
to five acres.

I nurtured each plant
as if it were my own child.
Three years before
they're bound for market.
Three years fervently
larding the beds
with manure, praying
for engorgement,
embonpoint,

for spears as rude
and round
and succulent
as fantasy allows.

My Battersea beauties,
forgive the blade
that cuts you
in your prime.
How strange the dialect
that carries you to market
as sparrowgrass.
Adieu, mes enfants.
New shoots
will claim my time.

LIVESTOCK

I
Mrs Nichol's Dairy
Liverpool Road, 1865

Each bolt to the head
shatters our bones.
City air thickens
deep with lowing,
as London turns Heifer,
mourns her lost calves.

They say it spread from my sheds
but Mr Baldwin and Mr Carvel's cows
brought it too – so keep your filthy stares.

I've lost ninety-three.
Lovely brown jerseys,
our best milker, fine big
black and whites.

More go each day;
one by one we drive
our heavy hearts down City Road
to short, wasteful deaths.
The growing pyre
watched by eyes
streaming with loss
and stench of carcass.

Soon there'll be no
swishing tails or gentle nudge
of a bull's nose, no nuzzling heads
or haunches to pat.

It's a bitter cud
we'll wash down with milk
not from London.

II
Cattle Herder's Wife
Holloway, c1811

We came to England from lush, green valleys,
drove our cattle onwards – Big Bess up front –
until this glittering sight from a-top the hill widens
our eyes at the greatness of city stretched before us;
horizon ready to be milked.

Nothing like home. Bigger than Cardiff.
We stand, looking, quiet 'cept snorts of cow breath,
my growing belly churning, Bess straining to join
eight thousand cows, add her fresh foaming squirts.

Such a sight - great grey teats full of gold coin
aching to spill on the floor. Quick! Get our pails
underneath and open our mouths.

III
Street Seller
Islington Green, 1575

Milk cheese and cream I cry.
Would you care to try?
Buy before I pass ye by.

Lac, caseus infans; three green cheeses
cream for custards or milk tankards
whatever you pleases!

Overflowing – pray let me tell –
like water fresh from the well.

Milk cheese and cream I cry.
Would you care to try?
Buy before I pass ye by.

Ready for drinking, not over-sodden,
like some lesser ones already forgotten.

Bonny children I hear you cry
for unchalked milk or clouted cream.
I've fresh butter for pastries –
a cake bread dream

Milk cheese and cream I cry.
Would you care to try?
Do buy before I pass ye by.

9 to 5

We took office jobs, boardrooms;
smashed avocados, ceilings.

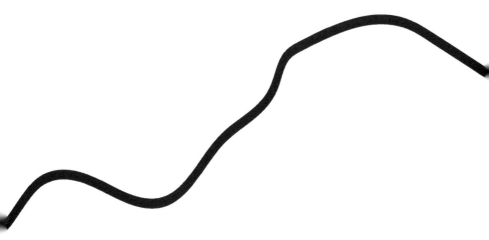

My feet trod
where others had trudged,
laboured, loved.

FOR ALL FOUNTAIN PENS

1. A Local Ponders Where Time Went
Drayton Park, 1960s

To find the factory's remains, I go –
Stephens' Ink and his inventive new way
of *indelible black that dries blue*, so
births, deaths, unions will not fade away.

My job there – one of the first girls – a mark
of endurance. All my endless bending
as we labelled bottles, barrels of dark
permanence, filled up for worldwide sending.

Liquid across oceans, and legends tell
shipwrecked survivors nil, 'cept Stephens' Ink.
Quills dipped, fountains full, ne'er an empty well.
But boom – this empire's dried, drawn to the brink

and demolition makes a splattered blot
of my past, and his nibs – *gone* – the whole lot.

2. A Newcomer Scratches the Surface
Gillespie Road, 2015

A huge factory, his nibs – the whole lot gone?
No sign of brickwork, barrel, inkwell, it's true.
Yet there's a community centre on
which his name proves that old's given way to new.

To find more traces of Inky's worldwide fame
into Stephens' home I dip and see displays
of his vast empire under museum glass – shame;
the impermanence of such glory days.

A closer look at historical endeavour shows
scant record of factory girls' lives – did they
fill bottles, design poster ads? Seems no one knows.
So I'll rectify that in verse form; printed out today

on A4 from my inkjet in CYMK black
and pin it up on 'X' marks the spot, like a memorial plaque.

For ALL fountain pens – Stephens' Ink advertising slogan accompanied
with an inkblot logo
Inky – Mr Stephens became affectionately referred to as Inky

WICKERS
Price's Candles, 1928

Quick with the hot needle
to pierce each nightlight.
Deft at threading the wick.
Swift to lam it in the tin.
Totting up as I go:
six dozen for one penny.

I've learnt to be quick
to pay my keep,
stash a few shillings
for powder and soap.

And though it's one step up from packing
you're still standing start to finish.
By early evening, I'm spark out
counting nightlights in my sleep.

So who'd complain, those days,
come high summer,
when heat warps wax by lunchtime
and we're laid off for the afternoon.

We leg it down to Latchmere Baths.
I'm first in, last out,
part mermaid, part stewed prune.

I'll feel the pinch on payday
but tonight I'll be dead to the world,
my dreams numberless, fluid, deep.

REGULAR SERVICE
Jones Brothers, Holloway Road (Haberdashery), 1890

Does Madam care for gloves today?
(*to hide your ring-less hand*)

They match your skin.
Calf (*skinned*)

Shall I ring it up to Sir's bill?
(*or has his missus got her beady
eye on that?*)

Beads? Next counter.
Follow me. Green.
Jade. Painted.
Tart… ra… zine feather
(*your nest while the going's good*)

Not today madam?
Then do call again
(*when I'm not serving*)

SACKED
Cook's Confectioners, Battersea Rise, 1923

I never pilfered, never dibbed
a wet finger in a sugar bag
for a sneaky suck.
All my roses turned out beautiful,
wedding-cake perfect.

But my legs don't take to sitting
hours on end. I'm shaking
the charleston on the metal topped table
showing off my donkey-kicks
when Mr Cook walks in.

He sends me packing
but I'll waltz straight into Lyons,
show them I can balance plates
on aeroplane arms,
shimmy between tables.

DODGING THE DOCTOR
The White Lead Works Factory, Islington, 1892

Our once-soft hands *snap* thin dried
white lead from metal sheets,
turn it into pigment snowstorm
to make paint that whitens
china plates, cups, our insides.
We're chalky with anaemia,
gums blue, constantly headachy.

It's our job they once said, for girls
didn't get poisoned like men.
But now a doctor visits regular,
warns us *Take a bath once a week.*
Any sign of sickness
we're sent home,
our pay docked.

To avoid diagnosis,
I drift silently in blizzard,
invisible in powder-fogged air,
clamber barefoot
up the drying scaffold,
hide at the top on rough planks.
Hup I go.

A 13-Year-Old Girl's To Do List
Secret Location, Islington, 1893

1. Lock the front door
put the crow on lookout at street-end
'case the police come a-knocking
with sledgehammers.

2. Uncle melts spoons.

3. Bill greases the real coins with tallow,
so collars won't stick and halves harden
around them, be put together easy.

4. Ma is on the cyanide dip,
smiling at electro plate magic
as it turns blue metal to silver.

5. Pa dries the mould, watching for hints
that the metal might fly.

6. Tom nips the gat with scissors
as a new shilling emerges, passes it on to me.

7. We'll hum and laugh as Tom goes too quick
or leaves me twiddling as a tease.

8. It's my turn to knerl the grooved edges
made ill-shaped by plaster of Paris,
until a fingernail won't snag.

9. Pass to Aunt Sal at her slumming post –
she'll dirty up the shine with lampblack and oil.

10. Make sure each fake looks like
it's been handled by many an eager finger
and come to us for cleaning, not making.

11. Meld on and on, a merry-go-round
of coin pieces, so clever in our fakery we itch
to pocket one or two.

12. Tonight's lot is already sold and wanted.

13. Ma says we can't be precious about our art.

Gat – the tell-tale neck of the channel through which the metal was poured
Knerl – the pattern on the sides of the coin
Slumming – smearing the bright metal with lampblack and oil

IN THE ETHER
Garratt Lane, 1931

Unskilled general labourer.
That's the box the census taker ticks.
Doesn't want to know the truth
about my job at Veritas, dipping mantles,
so the likes of him have gaslight of an evening
for reading their fancy books.

Unskilled general labourer.
Me and Flo and Gracie
we've perfected the rhythm of our work.
Lift a tray of mantles off the belt.
Place it in your tank.
Wind it right down
into that collodion stuff.
Let the hoods of knitted silk
soak a mo.   Don't   drift   off.
Draw the tray up
ever
        so
            slow.
Push it in the oven for baking.
Swing back to the belt
for another batch.

Unskilled general labourer.
All day long
me and Gracie and Flo
lift   place   wind down
        s   o   a   k

33

draw up   push   swing
skilled in this monotony,
dreaming of the flicks on Saturday
and gassing so we don't nod off.

By shift's end, we're numb to the stink.
So hold your nose, *Mister Census Taker*,
while you tick that box. *Unskilled general labourer.*
I don't give a damn what you think.

Collodion contains ether

Marking the Sheets
Apprentice Laundress, London Provincial, 1890s

The first job you learn,
a month shy of fourteen.

You stitch red cotton
into a piece of cloth,

perfect numbers 1 to 8,
letters ABC;

gain the superintendent's
nod of approval.

Then nine-hour days
marking the sheets,

the shirts, the unmentionables,
stitching household codes

into every unwashed garment,
all the bed-stripped linen,

your mind's eye blinkered
against intimacy.

In time, you'll learn washing
and starching, the calender

press and the goffering iron.
Already, you know the value

of women's work. Tuppence an hour.
Be thankful for the laundry roof

and dorm walls painted
with a fading truth:

Cleanliness is next to godliness.
Be grateful for the comfort

of the other girls,
for a tightening bond

you would not know to name
as camaraderie, for the skills

they teach in banter
and getting-on-with-it.

And when you wake before dawn
for the first time, a fistful of cramp

in your belly, staining the sheets,
helpless to staunch the flow –

fully orphaned – how you cling
to the quiet kindness of the matron

who fixes you up, brings tea,
tells you you're a woman now.

Everybody
OUT!

Colleagues call commercials
where women demonstrate
a cleaning product:
Two C's in a Kitchen.
Am I one of them?

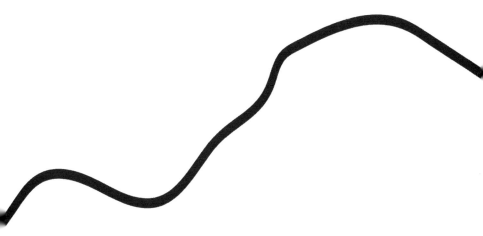

No hierarchy on the picket line.
We placard, joke, chant, chatter, long for hot tea.
The rest of the day blooms wide –
its promise our own making.

SHAME, SHAME, SHAME
*Sit-In at Decca's Colour TV Factory,
Ingate Place, 14th August 1975*

They lied to us. They lied with untranslated words.
Redundancy. Spit it out in Gujarati:નિરર્થકતા. We hear it as
futility. They translate us into *no job in two weeks.* નિરર્થકતા.
Our *insignificant* bodies occupy their factory. They nail up
the toilet doors. They send our food away. નિરર્થકતા. They
brand us with the stigma of *barrenness.* Together we've
assembled hundreds, thousands of colour TVs. Between
us, we feed dozens upon dozens of dependents. Why close
this factory? Why not a three-day week, like we see on
our black and white TVs in our crowded borrowed homes?
We are seventy strong. Our occupying bodies speak louder
than the words they didn't dare translate. Now, they will
hear us. Nationalise Decca's!

નિરર્થકતા. Nirarthakata – the Gujarati word for redundancy, which
carries a strong social stigma

41

OH I SAY, I'M STRIKING FOR FAIR PAY!
Outside Collins Music Hall, Islington Green, 1907

Ta-ra-ra boom de-ay
my pay went that a-way,
won't even cover
my do, re, mi, fa, sol, la ti ray
that's why we beg of you:
make our pay fair, today.

Hey, you, Sir – sneakin' round
to the artistes' door,
for a peak of ankle or even more,
go on listen to the second verse
yes, you bet – it's even worse:

Ribs poke through sequin le-o-tard,
you can play a tune on 'em nice an' hard –
ac-com-pa-ny the or-ches-tra;
like xylophones at the Dor-chester.

'Ere Officer, why should con-tor-tion-ists
bend over back-wards for did-dly squat?
Sand dancers scratch a living on broken toes
while the show on and on… and on… it goes?

Ta-ra-ra boom de-ay
driving meself into an ear-ly grave
dash from East Ham to St John's Wood
four or five times a day – if you fancy it,
don't do you an-y good.

Ta-ra-ra boom de-ree
how's a girl's to robe up with great ease
so she can disrobe on a fly-ing trapeze
when she ain't got no vis-i-ble means?
(Even Marie Lloyd sits among the peas, for beans.)

Hold my ha'penny, Sir, while I put on
this fake fur, blacken a false moustache
slick back curls, fall about like an arse.

I ply my trade to packed, swel-ter-ing houses
for a mea-sly wage, six music halls a day
from chorus line to top of the bill
– no wonder I'm so ill.

We bring hap-pi-ness to your door,
give you what you've been wait-ing for –
please help us keep the wolf from the door
pay us an extra shillin'
... or two... or three... ... or four!

Ta-ra-ra Boom-de-ay originally credited to Henry J Sayers 1891 revue Tuxedo, Boston Massachusetts. Became widely known by the version sung by Lottie Collins in London Music halls 1892.

A little of what you fancy does you good – Words and Music by Fred W. and George Arthurs – 1915, Performed by Marie Lloyd (1870-1922)

She sits among the cabbages and peas – sung by Marie Lloyd

THE GREAT ESCAPE

Headphones turned up, rug laid down,
sunny Sundays in the garden
drowning out helicopters, sirens,
Arsenal scoring at home.

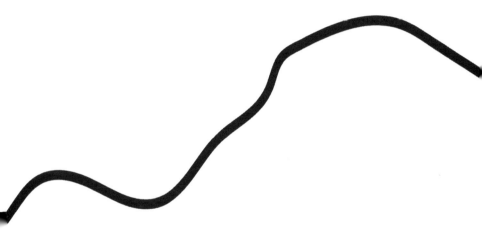

A park bench gardener,
I soak up the fruits
of others' everlasting labours.

HOLLYWOOD COMES TO HOLLOWAY
The Gaumont, 1949

But now I want to be a Yank
drawling out of the side of my lips

like Lauren. Looking up misty-eyed
like Betty. Swooning in Clark's arms

'cause he slapped me in the face then
kissed me like there's no tomorrow.

Saturday night we queue round the block
in kitten heels and headscarves. Push our

coins, saved-up from bingo winnings,
through the grill at the clerk with the quiff

and the easy leer, then *run* like teenagers
down to the front. Outside there are trams,

rain, kitchens, and three kids. But in the dark
there's red velvet, staircases like Scarlett's

and there's black and white instead of grey.
The love story lasts an hour, not *years*,

and The End is happy. Men light cigarettes
for you or draw down the moon. Tomorrow,

I'll style my hair like Joan's, drape over
the settee bought on HP, dream of the man

who doesn't leave his socks on the floor
or try it on when he's back from the boozer.

The man who tips his hat, says Ma'am not
Luv, walks us arm-in-arm, into the sunset.

Eloping in a Bread Basket
At the Foot of Canonbury Tower, c1570

Oh Father, would that I were born your son
not this lovesick maid
on the run in Augustinian-like silence,
choosing to scramble down knotted sheets,
grazing skin, heart a-pounding
instead of staying, doing your bidding
forsaking my lover – no – not even disinheritance
can force me to declare that it's over.

Oh Father, I give up:

32s 10d a year
All rents of customary tenants of 11s a year
The dovecotes
Orchards
Fixtures, fittings
Farmland in the north
A father's love
My home

Take it from me, Father.
I care not if you live up to your threat.
For, on his uppers tho' he may be,
my match is: Honest, True,
with a handsome ruff and a fine leg.
Is that him now, come to carry me off?

Oh Father, tho' I have had a soft landing
into pfffs of pastry, my skirts are adrift,
flour up my nose, loaves upon my head.
All because my sex does not speak to my sex.
Her Majesty Queen Elizabeth herself
dareth not recognise daughters as heirs.

Oh Father, your Majesty, my faithful pet dog,
the whole wide world and his mistress besides,
can't you all see: I crouch in yeast, ready to rise?

PERMITTED TO PLAY
Arsenal Football Stadium, Home End, 1991

Dad, when I grow up I will be
First Division, midfield, score
the winning goal. On this turf,
Arsenal Stadium, Gillespie Road.

Teacher says I'm better than the boys.
Dad, Dad, I can beat them on this pitch.
With you and mum eating hotdogs
in the red seats, waving scarves.

On telly, they only show the men's.
Dad, when can I play for Arsenal? When?

At time of going to print, Arsenal Women Football Club play at
Meadow Park, Borehamwood. They are permitted to play at Emirates
Stadium 'on occasion'.

ALL SHE DESIRES
Refreshment Kiosk, Battersea Park, Summer, 1895

A girl can dream.
She can dream all day
while serving teas
and clearing tables
and taking orders
from ladies wilting pleasantly
under shady trees,
their covetable bicycles
propped and resting
after so many circuits round the park.

A girl can dream
of how many miles she'd ride,
out to Richmond and beyond
into countryside and sootless air.
How boundless then her horizons.

So, off you go, ladies,
refreshed, aglow, tootling blithely
to your Mayfair homes.
This girl has to hoof it
up the Junction, weary of limb,
and longing for her very own
freedom machine.

Sandwiched between little sis and big 'un,
a girl can dream of spokes and pedals,
two flashing wheels,
the unstoppable momentum
of her journey out
into the world.

THE FEMALE GAZE

Leave knickers and socks wherever they fall,
no one to tell me what colour to paint the wall

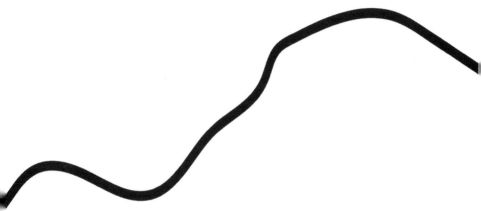

In the hairdresser's mirror
my teenage self glums back,
mouth cross-stitched against brute jests:
cheer up, love, might never happen!

DIDO BELLE SITS FOR HER PORTRAIT
Kenwood House, 1779

No corn-fed,
cotton-raised statue am I
nor decoration
picked for porcelain shine
to be cooed at like a pet;
I am a gift
of a mischief-maker
companion to this nearly-
sister by my side.

Draped in gold,
silk turban, feathers,
hooped earring, I'm a pearl
of the seas –
green as rain,
clean of plantation dust,
weaned on acres of meadow,
piano, needlecraft, wealth.

Father shipped me,
half-slave, across
waves of guilt –
a cargo of tea,
sugar, cotton,
coffee, rum,
fruit, wine,
tobacco, rape –

N

to an almost-
freedom,
this in between;
full-placed
in an artist's
composition yet
kept at the edge
of the real canvas.

BATTERSEA PRE-RAPHAELITE DIPTYCH

1. The Painter Marie Spartali Stillman
Remembers Her Family Home
1903

Lyrical, the light; and every room
a paradise of damask and crystal,
mahogany and oak; my youthful
psyche in rhapsodic dialogue
with *Baba's* old masters.

Daughter of the Greek diaspora,
I was born to nostalgia;
my mother's name synonymous
with euphoria, emblematic
of those halcyon days.

There on Lavender Hill,
my sister and cousins and I
graced the lawns,
London arrayed before us.

My father's villa a magnet
for bibliophiles and aesthetes.
The marbled halls echoed
with poetry, music, rhetoric –
such was my schooling – and *Baba*,
at the epicentre, orchestrating.

Behind the scenes, *Mama* dosed me
with nectar and balsam and myth;
her hypnotic chorus the alchemy
that cast me heroine
of my own story.

2. Euphrosyne Spartali to Her Daughter Marie
c1857

Koritsi mou, may you grow as tall
as a cypress, as strong
as a grain of rice.
Though men will weep
at your uncommon beauty,
idolise your sandalled feet,
your bee-kissed lips,
let not their idiocy govern you.

Rechristened as Muse,
hymned in paint as Hypatia,
Mnemosyne, Zoe – let your triumphs
be greater than these.
May your decades unroll
as a stretch of bare canvas
that you seize and autograph daily.

Your mother's tongue
baptises you Protagonist.
Break no bread with Tragedy.
Pepper your diet instead
with apricot, sesame,
sunlight, honey and fig.
And in the fullness of time
name your first son Michael,
for your father,
your daughter Effie
after me.

A River
Runs
Through It

Driving north again
over Blackfriars Bridge,
across Thames, above Fleet,
compelled back to the source.

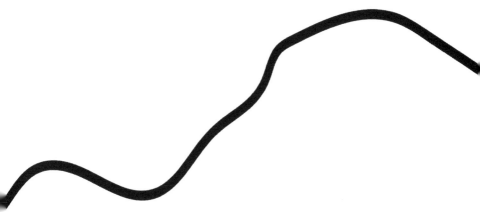

In all weathers, all moods,
the river holds my gaze,
creates connections.

GETTING HER LADYSHIP READY FOR THE FROST FAIR
Highbury Manor, 1814

She has requested my service
to keep her rightways up
for the tiptoe walk across plank,
over filthy frozen Thames,
and the slip-slide dance upon crackling ice,
until we reach thick sturdiness –
our noses and fingers frozen,
breath like icicles.

So I'll lace her stays tight,
wind her in woollen shawls
tether her chignon with eight pins
double-bow her bonnet with muslin.
All to admire a mighty elephant
of fearful size and strength.
They say it can kill a man.

On the ice, she'll send me
to fetch salted fish, sweetmeats,
gin. I'll urge her to stay north side.
She'll arch her brow
at such impertinence –
in secret, heartily glad
to have no need
of crossing south.

We'll link arms like sisters,
eyes agog at the grey giant
hoping it doesn't
flatten the lot of us –
for this is singular occasion
when I am no longer maidservant,
she, no longer mistress.

THAMES CROSSING, SECOND ATTEMPT
19th August 1861

start

b
a
l
a
farewell Battersea advancing step by practised step with my   n
c
e
|
p
o
l
e

hurrah! hurrah!
boo! take a ducking!
look at her go! man alice -   pleasure steamers
those skirts must weigh   boats   boats
a tonne! let me see!   skiffs
huzzah! steady - steady -   rowing boats
she's done it! bravo!   skiffs

72

finish: 7 minutes

on properly weighted rope this time I WILL reach Cremorne Gardens

will she? won't she?
look out - she's on her way!
what a strange get-up
rowing boats   *Albanian, you say? well I*
      boats   *never! such pluck! rather her*
    rivercraft   boats   *than me. here she comes!*
        skiffs   *ouch. what a crush! she's*
rowing boats   *made it! praise the Lord!*

WHAT *YOU* STARING AT?

I'm paying for my own meal
like a fucking hero.

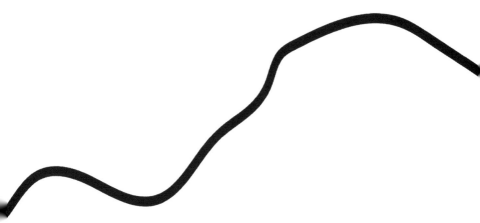

I change my name
dye my hair
risk red lipstick
learn to love my cyclist's legs.

KICKING BACK IN THE BLACK HOUSE
Above the Shop, Holloway Road, 1969

No coloureds. No Irish.
Pretty tune of knuckle and slap.
Two fingers in mi face –
curse, threats, *go back.*

But I cahn tone down.
Cahn submit. Was invited.
Promised a new start;
golden like Alice's
Olympic medal.

Battered, mi wash up
on Red Mike's jagged rocks,
shivering in sandals an' dress.

Him Panther strength howls
across rooftop, snarls us
together – afro, pot, free love.
World Cup. Who we
cheer fe now? Which side mi on?

Year after year
cub grow tall and willowy
in concrete rain estate,
play with others, give birth
to mixed seeds
settle here and there
here or there.

On the Way to See The Sex Pistols Play at the Hope and Anchor
Upper Street, '77

What you staring at
Never seen black eye
shadow before,
lips painted black,
wet with spit?

Never heard a girl's tongue
kiss the air with profanity?

Never fancied legs smattered
with fishnet rips?
The shaved sides of head?

Tut and gripe all you want –
it's music to ears
punctured with safety pins;
means my sexed-up
nonconformity hits you
like a flob of anarchy.

I'm not Sid's girl.
I study art up the road,
sharpened by paint fumes,
bleach, razor blades.

You can't fight.
Hundreds of me
pogo in basement gigs
thrashing against
your label of 'Woman' -
what you want us to be
– *you robots.*

Go on, take a good look.
We're pretty in black,
mother, daughter, sister, Punk.

MARY KINGLSEY ARRIVES WITHOUT A HUSBAND
Dinner Party, Highbury, 1893

I travel as far as I please alone.
Not missionary wife. No wedding ring.
In my own canoe I feel at home.

Tropical sunsets beat Islington's gloom.
Grey rain, parents dead – dull notes to sing.
Better to travel across Africa on my own.

Studying people, reporting home,
until *Freedom for all in our colonies* we bring
I'll keep on travelling afar alone.

My own canoe; no husband, alone.
New woman? It's not a Suffrage thing.
When I travel upstream I feel most at home.

Strong roots pull me to London loam.
Frighten off rats with the monkey under my wing.
Male-only science? *Pah!* I'll break in alone.

High collars, petticoats don't make it easy to roam.
But discovery, learning, moving are my thing –
so I'll travel as far as I please, alone.
Just as I am I feel at home.

LADY CYCLIST
Summer 1895

Brazen in bloomers
    I weave through the throng
        streaming south
        over the river
    into the lush cool
of Battersea Park.
        The height of daring.
    Wed to my saddle
        I own the carriageway,
        proving my balance
        as I lean – tilt – sway;
    my quickening pins glory
in their rational garb.

I swish – whoosh – slalom
    between wayward Mayfair ladies,
        Chelsea's untamed daughters;
        the safety bicycle
    our new bosom friend.
I care not a fig
    for my flushing cheeks
        my runaway hair
        the flash of azaleas
    nor the gentlemen who stare.
I am rider and vehicle
    racing full pelt
        lap after lap
            after lap

NATURE/NURTURE

A sleuthing city fox, nose down,
appears as if hallucination
at my late-night work-wired bus stop.

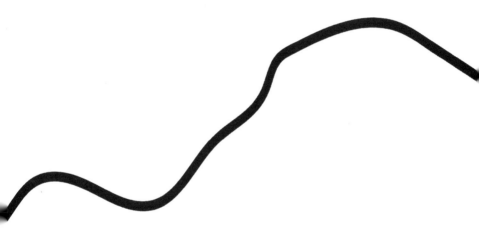

I never heard birds outside my window
until the trees grew.

LAVENDER HARVEST
c1740

Labourer's hands, these,
chafed by the stems I snap,
cracked and bleeding
by morning's end.

I bend between the beds,
girdled by an ache so like
my monthlies, my inmost self

oozing into the godless soil.
Beneath unpretty petticoats
my knees click,
my hips lock; balance

knocked by this tricky basket,
heavy with flowers,
awkward twin to the child
I've yet to bear.

I sneeze ceaselessly,
nostrils swollen by fine dust,
blue haze. I long for white,

for colourless odourless sheets,
a full night's sleep. Bees
pollinate my dreams,
hound my every waking hour.

Lavender's for healing, they say.
Who'll pluck me from this field,
rid me of this purpling stench?

PAYING FOR THE POOR HOUSE
Liverpool Road, 1732

Our debt of room
must be scratched out
by untwisting rope,
unpicking heavy tarred
cables into tiny fibres.

This oakum will
swell between boards,
wedge cracks –
make ships
watertight again.

The kids are scattered,
our lives tangled.
With cracked
hessian hands I grasp
at threads, free
a few small strands
of jute and hemp
from this blackened mess.

He Was a Lovely Boy
Somewhere on the Estate, Essex Road, 1969

My lad, my son, my blood.
Brought him up nice, polite.

His second birth tore me apart.
Both halves twinned together –

could've ripped them in two
with my teeth, but this one

kept the peace, stayed respectful,
never swore. Class. Stuck to his code:

just his bare hands grappling
in the back rooms of pubs.

Knives or guns?
You choose you lose.

Divided, my heart still leaps
when police sirens call.

For a moment I forget
we laid him to rest

in his new suit
dressed nice for his old mum.

NEIGHBOURS
Stewart's Lane, 1930s

Beecham's Pills should do the trick,
I tell her. *Take 'em*
when he's down the pub
and the kids are tucked up.

She pulls the door to,
cradling her cup of sugar.

Take 'em with a mug of hot gin.
That'll ease yer worries.

They're behind on the rent
like most of our street
her third nipper not long weaned
and herself peaky as a skinned rabbit.

Just pray it don't start
on the tram in to work.
It comes on heavy. Been through it meself.
Three times. Each one worse than the last.

Thanks, June, she whispers.
Lets herself out, clutching the cup.

Next time she knocks
I get my sugar back.
We have a right old moan
about our husbands.
I don't ask. She doesn't say.

An Easy Evening's Work
Gypsy Encampment, No-Man's-Land, near
Wandsworth Road, Winter 1864

I prick my ears to the snarl of dogs.
Mr Borrow is on our ground;
that scribbler who mines the Romany life,
after tales for his book, I'll be bound.

Through the mud he treads t'wards my bender.
I've a hunch my luck is in.
My kettle's a-simmer, and so is my tale.
When he doffs his hat I begin:

Three score years and ten or more
I've roamed these parts about.
The heaviest man I can easily hoick –
you'll've heard of me no doubt.

For I'm Charlotte Cooper, wronged yet faithful wife
of Jack, the fighting Gypsy,
who, 'neath dappling trees on mossy beds,
in Loughton Forest wooed me.

Our courtship blazed with fisticuffs
and for every blackened eye
I socked my Jack right back. Once wed,
he'd nothing me deny.

With every fight my husband won
I garnered silks and lace.
A bonny son I bore 'fore long, and love it was
we carted place to place.

What name has she but harlot that stole
my Jack from me. Bewitched him
to abandonment and worse—to blanket-theft!
Those nights were cold and grim.

But grimmer still the day he stood
in dock and fessed up to a crime
that harlot done. Van Diemen's Land
his fate, to toil ungodly time.

How long the years endured since
and every suitor spurned
for, steadfast and true, I'm expecting yet
my husband Jack's return.

Kind sir, you seem a learned man,
I say, and bashful-like admit:
Only fortunes can I read. This letter here –
pray tell me what Jack's writ.

A tatty paper scrap I pluck
from my meagre treasure hoard
and Mr Borrow declaims those tired old lines
I've had read to me oft before:

My dearest wife, my Charlotte true,
how I miss your fierce embrace.
By your side I'll lie again, I swear,
once my fortune in gold I have made.

My eyes feign tears, I puff my breast
and make as if his words provoke
a sigh so heartfelt, so profound, as to inflame
the brazier's dying coke.

Mr Borrow, overcome by pity, pours
silver into my thirsty palm.
My husband can hang for all I care.
And if I've 'broidered my tale, where's the harm?

War –
What Is It Good For?

The cats are vying for the tiny patch of sun
on next-door's flat roof again.

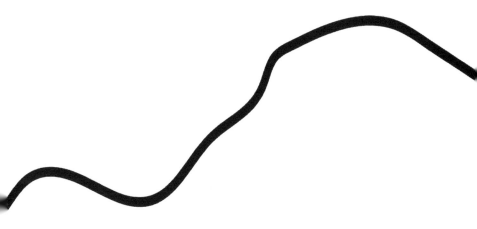

Talha Ahsan is home.
Shaker Aamer is free.
The US Embassy
has opened its doors in Nine Elms.

WHAT DID YOU DO IN THE WAR GRANNY?
Social Housing, Mackenzie Road, 1970

These are the hands that dandled your mum
on my knee, later you too, held hot soldering
irons, welded casing onto bullets so steady and true
the factory foreman called my work *exemplary.*

These are the eyes that stop pots boiling
over, and darted left, right, left, right
checked for imperfect parts on conveyor belts
over and over and over and over.

These are the arms sweeping out the backyard
that turned berry brown from hours of sun
through forklift windows while working hard
packing grenades, shells, guns.

These are the fingers that sew buttons and hems
but once earned a weekly wage only just short
of the men's, then waved at the barman *it's my
shout girls*, untied my hair, shook out gunpowder, curls.

This is the wedding ring I was made to take off
before entering the factory in case it got caught
and stopped the war effort, our hard work for naught.
It's not left my hand since the last day I clocked off.

These are the stories your old Gran will tell you
and there are ones I'll keep buried inside –
those things that I missed and the things that I didn't,
and how when the men came back home I cried.

CLIPPIE, TOP DECK
Route 19, 1917

I swear to God–when all this ends
you won't see *me* back in service.
I'm done with hours on my knees
scrubbing someone else's floors,
mumbling *yes ma'am, no ma'am*
to *Madam Balham.*

I won't be cooped below stairs
when I've had the run of London.
Never used to hardly cross the river.
Now it's ten times a day, all weathers,
and I'm singing out the stops:
Clapham Junction!
               Battersea Bridge!
                           Beaufort Street!

A plash of rain don't bother me–
reminds me I'm alive.
And every swing of Route 19
is patterned in my brain.

Give me a starless night
or choking fog
and I'll still not miss a stop
between Piccadilly and Finsbury Park
nor southbound far as Tooting Bec.

Punching tickets top deck, sleet stinging my cheeks,
still beats mangling milady's sheets and towels.
But if she begged on bended knee for my return?
No.
Whatever peace brings, from here on in
I'm polishing nothing but my own boots.
Step up now.
       Hold tight.
           Ding ding! Ding ding!

THE COOK SISTERS CONTEMPLATE A FINAL TRIP TO NAZI GERMANY
Twin Bedroom, 24 Morella Road, August 1939

Are you awake, Louise?
Wide as anything, Ida.
This time last night…
… we were on board the ferry
safe in our cabin
the hell of Frankfurt behind us.

Then off you went to work
straight from Liverpool Street
as if nothing had happened.

My handbag still ached
with Frau Liebermann's diamonds
and Herr Götz's pleas
all those desperate stories.

When I got home
Mother was in the kitchen
making pastry.
Little puffs of flour
rose in the sunlight
and I realised
there were no swastikas
flying in our street.
Praise be!

I burst into tears
the gaunt faces of the last two days
welling up in me.
Poor, dear Ida. And Mother
simply went on making pastry.
Isn't she marvellous!

Wonderful. In no time
I was my old self again.

Dear God, Louise, we daren't risk
going over there again…
but if there's a chance
to help one more person
one more family
before war breaks out
then we must… *we will.*

Their voices though…
I don't think they'll ever leave us, Ida.
Remember Ponselle as Norma,
thrilling us at Covent Garden?

Ah yes, Rosa! Clear as a bell.
She's singing to me now.
She's singing to us.
There's always Rosa.
Yes, there'll always be Rosa.

Louise?
Yes, Ida?

Goodnight. *Goodnight.*
Sweet dreams. *Sleep tight.*

AT 65, MISS LANCASTER IS STILL AT THE WHEEL
North Side, Clapham Common, June 1947

You can blame Hitler.
Cut my teeth
in the Blitz,
thundering fire engines
through blazing blackout
from Nine Elms
to Balham
and all smouldering routes
in-between.

Found my calling
in the driver's seat.
When peace broke out,
I opted for a hackney license,
my own limousine.

I'll ferry whoever flags me;
judge no one.
Blabbers and blubbers
spill their guts
in my roaming confessional.
I train my eyes on the road,
whistle as I listen,
accept their fare
as absolution.

Then on
into the quick quick   slow
of London traffic;
foot over the brake, ready
for the next lost soul.

The title comes from a headline in the South London Press

KNITTING FOR SPAIN IN THE PEOPLE'S BOOKSHOP
Lavender Hill, 12th December 1936

In the window we sit
casting on, counting stitches,
while the powers that be
sit on their hands
pleading non-intervention.

Click-clack of needles muffles
rat-tat of fascist guns

We are knitting as our mothers
and grandmothers knitted
but not for our husbands and sons
       not yet.

Slip one, knit one, pass the slipped stitch over
Mosley's thugs aren't welcome here

We are knitting for our brothers
and sisters in Spain
fighting the same fight to
Save London! Save Madrid!

We are knitting a convoy
of garments. Balaclavas
and cardigans fall from our needles
burdened with history.

Numb fingers, numb thumbs
Gloves for brave Republicans

We are knitting to save their lives
    To save our lives.

Knit one, purl one, stitch two together
Not for me, not for you, but for us
Knit one, purl one. No pasarán!

Not for me, not for you, but for us – Battersea motto

WE DON'T NEED NO EDUCATION

Ignore your sat nav.
I know these streets
with my eyes shut.

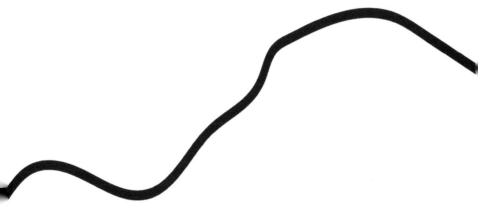

Scattered names took hold,
tenacious as buddleia
on a brick viaduct.

On Being Taught by Mary Wollstonecraft
Newington Green, Late 1780s

Her words were diamonds.
I can see her still, greeting a brisk
Good Morning girls
as we filed past, her fabrics
scented with classroom and ideas –
we twenty girls; raw rubies
she'd unearthed, ready to be polished,
delivered into cut-glass timetable
until our lustres started to shine,
dim facets almost glinted.

Nights sent us whispering into dorms –
'Had she really meant *such and such*?'
'Did she think it was possible?'
'Was she a bit touched in the head?'
Then we'd shush, afraid of our thoughts
about this woman who drove us towards
betterment in spite of ourselves.

She *believed.* Who were we with our
un-inked pages to be more clear-eyed
than our teacher? We were daughters
of Rational Dissent. Heiresses to the fabled
'just and egalitarian' future.
But what part can us girls play except
that which Government and our King decree?

All year, twenty heads bent;
sharpened pencils scratching
the surface until blunt from trying
Then our school doors locked – Mistress W
was forced to close. We scattered,
back to where she'd found us.
We tried to shine; at least I know I did.
I shone as much as I could.

ON THE MARRIAGE OF CATHERINE BOUCHER TO
WILLIAM BLAKE
St Mary's Church, Battersea, 18th August 1782

If there are children
I will tell them of his wooing:
how he pummelled his breast
and spoke his jilted tale
to my unschooled ear –
this, our first meeting –
and from my pity drew his new,
his true love. We two souls
recognised our equal.

Now, within the year,
we stand before God,
yards from the river
whose rising and falling
lullabied my infancy;
my nosegay undercut
by the dank hint
of reed beds. Above us
sunbeams ripple and bob.
We say our vows
bathed in a splendour of light.

And when he signs his name –
William Blake – in the register
I believe this to be true,
unable to decipher
those marks that flow
so swiftly, serpent-like,
from his pen. This X

I make, crooked, unfamiliar,
symbol of my freely given hand,
he swears he'll take and soon
have learnt me how to read and write.
To sign my own proud name:
Catherine Blake.

DEEDS NOT WORDS

Visitor – the ugliness
of the Holloway Road
is mine to slate,
but don't *you*
dare say anything bad
about it.

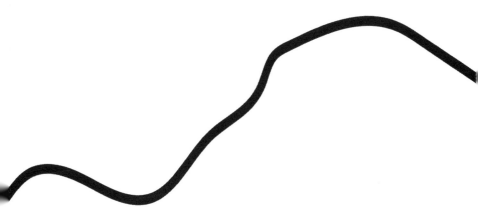

Woke up to find
I'd lived here half my life
Felt the pull of community.
Began to dig. Began to sow.

.

WHAT'S MRS DESPARD EVER DONE FOR US?
A Nine Elms Woman Speaks Up, December 1918

Boots for our barefoot sons.
The Despard Boys Club, what saved
my Alf from too much mischief.
Our Catholic Mothers group for tea,
chit-chat and 'nutritional advice'.
Soup kitchens when the men were laid off,
on strike, or called up to war.
Milk puddings for the little ones. And now,
at twice my age, she stands for Parliament
to fight our corner there. Husbands, sons –
we'll chivvy you to the ballot box.
We'd vote for Mrs Despard, if we could.

CAT AND MOUSE
Holloway Prison, 1913

They wait for the bruising to fade
from purple, green, yellow to white,

for elbow marks rammed into rib and shin
to fade, for a pinioned chest – made free

of corset – to cast off knee welts, for gums
to bud skin torn by metal jaws,

for cheeks to hide histories of hands
that forced open a mouth to gag

on rubber pipe. This waiting affords me
respite at home, soft boiled eggs, a glimpse

of headlines. Then they'll start again. But we,
my sisters, we will wait no more.

CHEERS!

My round, our local, *this*;
my family of friends.

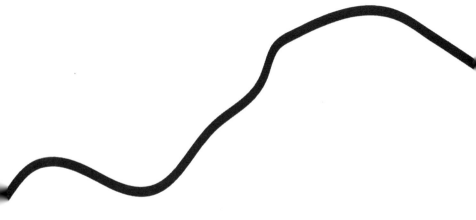

I stagger home in the small hours
drunk on London
drunk on belonging.

Battersea Women's Pub Outing
June 16th 1947

We never stop laughing
there's Queenie in her bloomers
clowning as we crowd onto the bus
a jolly clink of beer bottles
getting our thirst up early
lively banter from the off
the biggest cheer for trusty Beryl
jingling our year's stashed subs
in a chamber pot
    wave bye-bye to our homely patch
of bombed-out streets
chanting *Margate-here-we-come!*
Driver Dave a dream to tease
pays us back with swerves and jolts
that jiggle-tickle greater squeals
from hyperventilating bosoms
nearly burst our sides if not for corsets
    refuelling at each wayside stop with beer
linking arms and voices in rollicking singalong
kicking our legs high
such larks!
    let loose in Margate
we rampage every ride
Little Lottie roars so much
she heaves her dinner up
soon as she's off the Big Dipper
takes our ribbing in her stride
knocks back another beer
with a sparkle in her eye
    we never want the day to end

the sun to set
as we scuff sand
and wriggle-giggle out of stockings
and plunge our feet into Kentish foam
then gorge on fish 'n chips
and Marj cracks us up saying *batter's better in Battersea*
she isn't wrong
      the whole way back
we keep our spirits up with song
and natter and booze 'cos
after the war we thought would never end
after the winter we thought would never end
we mean to have fun.
And didn't we have fun!

A Lock-In with Widow Liquorish
Peacock Inn, Upper Street, 1670s

Resolved to head home? *Naaaah!*
Pray do 'ave one more.
I've closed the shutters,
bolted the door.

Stay for a nightcap.
There's my well-stocked cellar to rely on.
Who needs the largeness of The Angel?
Or the stinking back yard of the White Lion?

The Ale here's hearty, and it's strong again.
It ain't watered down,
like The Pied Bull's –
not now me old man has gone.

Or what say you to sister botanicals?
Get mightily juniper-juiced
on nature's medicinals.
It's today's batch, straight from a local still.

Sup a measure or two by my roaring fires.
Warm yer cockles, rosy yer parts.
It ain't for nothing they call me
the *Lady of the eight hearths.*

Friend – even if you're down on yer luck
there ain't no danger of an empty glass.
Widow Liquorish
won't throw you out on yer arse.

Rest awhile m'dear.
See how the candles flicker
like jewels, the liquor flows like the New River!
Ah sweetheart – rest yer 'ead.

~~

'Ere wake up! The next tide of coaches
has washed up on my shores.
Go on – git out – it's two of the cock's crow.
The new lot are coming; it's time for you to go.

THE AUTHORS

JOOLZ SPARKES

Joolz Sparkes is a member of the collective, Malika's Poetry Kitchen, has featured at Ledbury Poetry Festival and was poet-in-residence at Leicester Square tube station. Shortlisted for the Bridport Poetry Prize in 2010, she is published in magazines such as Magma, South Bank Poetry, Great Weather for MEDIA, Shooter Literary Magazine and online at Ink Sweat & Tears.

'As a student and young adult, I lived in many boroughs of London, but Islington is the one that has claimed me as one of her own. It's only since working on this joint project that I've realised the sheer volume of women who have lived in my local area but whose lives have gone unheard and unrecorded over the centuries.

Where are the statues, the blue plaques, the names in reference books, the social histories? I had to delve deep, listen to ghosts, discover and imagine, search hard for signs of the women who've struggled, laughed, scraped by, thrived, dreamt, and left their traces in London's shifting clay. It should not be so hard to find them.'

The Authors

Hilaire

Hilaire has several poems published in Emma Press anthologies – Aunts, Age, Mildly Erotic Verse; and in magazines such as Brittle Star, ARTEMISpoetry and South Bank Poetry. She was poet-in-residence at Thrive Battersea in 2017 and is one of three featured poets in Triptych Poets: Issue One from Blemish Books which showcases 18 of her poems.

'I knew nothing about Battersea when I first moved to the area, and for many years my orientation was towards the West End and cultural life outside my immediate surroundings.

I always loved Battersea Park, the derelict Power Station, and the blue gasometers I could see from my flat. Then things started to change, rapidly, right on my doorstep. I began to take more note of my neighbourhood, exploring the nearby streets; walking, looking up, wondering; what was here before, who lived here before?

Soon I was raiding my library for local history books, and excitedly discovering Battersea's rich and radical past. I had to dig deeper to find the voices and experiences of Battersea's women, and too often there's very little trace. How much of our shared history have we lost?

I'm inspired by the women I've come across in the course of this project, and I'll keep on digging.'

NORTH

LIVESTOCK
In 1865, cattle plague wiped out most of London's cows. The outbreak is reported to have started at Mrs Nichols Dairy, Liverpool Road, Islington, from infected cattle recently brought into the country.

FOR ALL FOUNTAIN PENS
I spotted the remains of a building in a local nature reserve (Gillespie Park) and discovered that it's all that's left of Stephens' Ink factory. Henry Stephens invented indelible blue ink that dried black, which quickly became favoured worldwide. The Treaty of Versailles, bringing a formal end to World War I, was signed using Stephens' Ink, and Stephens' products accompanied Captain Robert Scott on the ill-fated Terra Nova Expedition to reach the South Pole.

REGULAR SERVICE
The six-storey Jones Brothers department store opened on the Holloway Road in 1899 and became a stylish and much-loved shopping venue. 1927 the shop became one of the Selfridge Provincial Stores. Following its closure in 1990 the building became occupied by a conference centre and shop, with hints of its grandeur remaining such as an arched glass doorway and red brick detailing.

DODGING THE DOCTOR
Samuel Walker built a tower mill at the White Lead factory at Rosemary Branch, Islington in 1786 with another in 1792. In lead factories during this time it was thought that women didn't get poisoned like the men. This practice of giving women the most dangerous job continued until 1895 when the Women and

Factories Act changed the laws around working conditions.

A 13-Year-Old Girl's to Do List

The art of coin counterfeiting, known as Coining carried the death penalty in the 1700s, yet girls as young as 14 were an integral part of this dangerous and arduous task, alongside their whole family. The punishment for women counterfeiters was burning at the stake, whereas men were hung.

Oh, I Say, I'm Striking for Fair Pay!

Collins Music Hall stood on the south side of Islington Green until the 1950s. In 1907 a theatrical dispute took place between music hall employees, stage artistes and London theatre proprietors due to lack of pay, perks being scrapped and an increase in working hours and matinée performances. Popular entertainers were active on the picket lines outside London and provincial theatres, including Marie Lloyd who also staged a benefit event with an all-female billing.

Hollywood Comes to Holloway

I used to live five minutes away from the Holloway Odeon and have watched hundreds of films there. I love its art deco outline against the sky as you head north along the grubby Holloway Road. I discovered that it was formerly called the Gaumont and was one of over 40 cinemas to have opened in Islington since film's invention in 1895. It has stood on the corner of Tufnell Park Road and Holloway Road N19 since 1938 and is still a working cinema to date.

Eloping in a Bread Basket

Canonbury Tower was part of a manor house built in the early 1500s by the Priory of St Bartholomew. From 1570 until 1610 it was owned by Sir John Spencer, who became Lord Mayor of London. His daughter Elizabeth became betrothed to William Compton, and Sir John strongly opposed the match. Legend has it that Elizabeth was smuggled out in a breadbasket and carried away by her betrothed so that they could elope.

PERMITTED TO PLAY

I live within a stone's throw of the Emirates Stadium and assumed that the women's team also played there. I discovered that most of their home matches are at Meadow Park, in Borehamwood, Hertfordshire. Founded in 1987 by Vic Akers, Arsenal Women (formerly Arsenal Ladies Football Club) won their first major honour, the Women's League Cup in 1991-92. Later in 1992 they won promotion to the FA Women's Premier League.

DIDO BELLE SITS FOR HER PORTRAIT

Born into slavery, Dido Elizabeth Belle was brought by her grandfather William Murray, 1st Earl of Mansfield, from Africa to England, where she was brought up at Kenwood House, Hampstead as a member of the household. A painting of her and her white half-sister hangs in Kenwood House, traditionally attributed to German artist Johann Zoffany, but since reattributed to Scottish artist David Martin. Until the early 1990s, it was simply known as The Lady Elizabeth Murray.

GETTING HER LADYSHIP READY FOR THE FROST FAIR

The last time the Thames froze over in 1814 a huge Frost Fair was held upon it, and lasted four days. An elephant was paraded across it as an attraction below Blackfriars Bridge. In Highbury at this time a great house stood on Highbury Hill.

KICKING BACK IN THE BLACK HOUSE

A pub on the Holloway Road has been a local landmark for many years, opening and shutting under new guises. I was intrigued to find out that the rooms above the pub hold an even more interesting history. In the 1960's the charismatic, self-styled political leader, Michael Freitas (who became known as Michael X) rented a rambling warren of rooms above three shops, which became a safe space and second home for young Afro-Caribbean men and women to hang out.

On the Way to See The Sex Pistols Play at the Hope and Anchor

As an ex-punk/goth, I was excited to discover that the Hope and Anchor pub was host to one of the Sex Pistols few live gigs in 1977. That same year, Islington Arts factory was founded, offering art classes at a low cost to anyone with a 'facility to express and experience art'.

Mary Kingsley Arrives Without a Husband

Explorer Mary Kingsley was born in Islington. She travelled solo at a time when women had to be chaperoned everywhere. I was particularly struck by reports that she distanced herself from feminism or 'new woman' as it was called in her day. Mary was intensely interested in different cultures and even discovered three new types of fish in the Amazon river. She wrote many papers and essays, one of which she was not allowed to read at a public event and had to ask a male colleague to read it for her.

Paying for the Poor House

The Borough of Islington had many Poor Houses. One of them, sited on Liverpool Road, was recorded as being of a marginally higher standard than most, with an infirmary and plant pots on each landing. Inmates were put to work picking oakum. It's now a multi-million-pound flat complex just around the corner from the former residence of former Prime Minister, Tony Blair.

He Was a Lovely Boy

With the Kray twins and their mother Violet just up the road in Hackney, Islington has been home to notorious families like the Nashes, the Regans and the Smiths, and has a history of gang crime. The perpetrators, and victims of this crime, are mostly young men and teenage boys.

WHAT DID YOU DO IN THE WAR GRANNY?
In 1916 an ammunitions factory opened in Brewery Road, Islington, where women helped the war effort by packing shells and handling explosives. That area of Islington still has big warehouses interspersed with social housing created in areas flattened by bomb damage and urban redevelopment.

ON BEING TAUGHT BY MARY WOLLSTONECRAFT
At the age of 24, Mary Wollstonecraft opened an innovative boarding school for girls in Newington Green in 1784. It lasted a year. Later in 1786, she wrote a short tract entitled Thoughts on the Education of Daughters, based on her time at the school.

CAT AND MOUSE
Whenever I used to tell people that I lived in Holloway, they'd often joke that I 'must have been let out for the day'. Now decommissioned and being redeveloped into flats, HMS Prison Holloway became female-only in 1903. Suffragette Janie Terrero who had been caught window smashing, was sentenced to four months in Holloway. Janie – like many Suffragettes – went on hunger strike. The authorities, fearing that Suffragettes might die from starvation, force-fed them as part of the Cat and Mouse act.

A LOCK-IN WITH WIDOW LIQUORISH
I didn't hear the words 'lock-in' until I was in my 20s when drinking with friends in a pub on the Essex Road. Although I soon came to realise that lock-ins happen nationwide, it's a term that I still associate with London's exciting nightlife and drinking culture. The Peacock Inn stood at no 11 Upper Street from 1564 and in the 1670s was recorded as having eight hearths and being run by a widow Liquorish. The Peacock is mentioned in Charles Dickens' Nicholas Nickelby and Tom Brown's School Days, it also features in an 1823 painting by James Pollard.

Visit the London Undercurrents blog for more background information londonundercurrents.wordpress.com

SOUTH

FIRST CROP
There's a pub on the corner of Battersea Park Road and Falcon
Road called The Asparagus, which I always thought was an
odd name for a local boozer. But as I researched the history
of Battersea I discovered it was the first place in Britain
where asparagus was grown. It's thought it was introduced by
Huguenot refugees.

WICKERS
Price's Candle Factory used to be one of the largest employers
in Battersea, and certainly the largest single employer of female
workers. One of the jobs undertaken by young women when
they started, aged 13 or 14, was putting the wicks into
nightlights. This was paid as piecework.

SACKED
Many of the women interviewed in For Love & Shillings, by Jo
Stanley and Bronwen Griffiths, recalled the circumstances of
leaving their job, as well as the detail of the day-to-day work.
One account struck me in particular and inspired this poem.

IN THE ETHER
Gas lighting was still in use in many households in the first
half of the 20th century. There were four gas mantle factories
in Wandsworth, including Veritas, and the workforce was
predominantly female.

MARKING THE SHEETS
There were a large number of commercial laundries in Battersea
in the late 19th and early 20th centuries. Girls aged 13 or 14,
starting out in their first job, often lived above the laundry, and
were supervised by a matron. The first task new recruits learnt
was 'marking the sheets' – stitching a combination of letters
and numbers onto each item received by the laundry so as to
identify which household it belonged to.

144

Shame, Shame, Shame

I chanced across a reference to a sit-in by Asian women workers at a local factory when I was searching Wandsworth Libraries' online catalogue. The short report published by Wandsworth Council for Community Relations revealed this was not a dispute on the same scale as the Grunwick strike, as I had briefly imagined. The sit-in lasted just over 7 hours from the evening of 14th August 1975 until the early hours of the following morning. But there were several factors I found compelling – the women were mostly Ugandan Asian refugees, and the company had not thought it worth providing English language classes as, in their view, 'when their English improves, they tend to leave'.

All She Desires

In the summer of 1895 there was a cycling craze amongst middle and upper-class women, who flocked to both cycle and socialise in Battersea Park. At that time, bicycles were beyond the means of poorer people.

Battersea Pre-Raphaelite Diptych

In one of the first local history books I read, there was a photo of a villa on Lavender Hill called The Shrubbery, accompanied by a short note stating that the villa had been leased in 1865 to a Greek merchant, Michael Spartali, whose daughters had modelled for Dante Gabriel Rossetti amongst others. I soon discovered that the younger daughter Marie, as well as being a renowned beauty and Pre-Raphaelite muse, was also a successful artist in her own right, enjoying a long and productive career. The Shrubbery still stands, though without the large grounds that surrounded it at the time the Spartalis lived there.

Thames Crossing, Second Attempt

I first came across a mention of the Victorian tightrope walker, sometimes referred to as the 'Female Blondin', in a slim local history booklet. The short account only relates her first, unsuccessful, attempt to cross from Battersea Bridge to Cremorne Gardens. Further research revealed that she made a second, successful, attempt a few days later. Her real name, according to the Oxford Dictionary of National Biography, was Selina Young. She was also known as Pauline Violante. Charles Blondin was a French acrobat who had crossed the Niagara Gorge on tightrope several years before.

Lady Cyclist
Battersea Park was a favourite place for women to gather and practise what was regarded as a rather risqué activity during the cycling craze of summer 1895. There was a concurrent movement advocating 'rational dress' for women, including bloomers for cycling.

Lavender Harvest
When I started researching my local area, I was surprised to learn that, before industrialisation, large areas of Battersea were covered with lavender fields. Traces of this history remain in street names such as Lavender Hill and Lavender Sweep.

Neighbours
Before the NHS, working class women had virtually no access to birth control, so had to rely on each other for advice. I drew on accounts in The midwife's tale, by Billie Hunter and Nicky Leap, to convey some of the harsh reality of women's struggle to control their fertility before contraception was widely available.

An Easy Evening's Work
In the 19th century, Romany families used to camp during the winter on unclaimed land in Wandsworth. The writer George Borrow recorded his visits to the camp in his book Romano Lavo-Lil, including an account of an extraordinary-sounding woman, Charlotte Cooper.

Clippie, Top Deck
During the First World War a lot of women left domestic service to become bus conductors, who were known colloquially as Clippies.

146

At the end of the war, their licenses to work as conductors were revoked, but most did not return to service.

THE COOK SISTERS CONTEMPLATE A FINAL TRIP TO NAZI GERMANY

It was at a Battersea Society talk that I first encountered the fascinating story of Ida and Louise Cook. They were opera-mad spinster sisters, who lived modestly in the family home at Morella Road for most of their lives. And who also happened to help at least 29 Jewish people escape Nazi Germany before the outbreak of the Second World War. Ida was also one of Mills & Boons most successful authors.

AT 65, MISS LANCASTER IS STILL AT THE WHEEL

I was scrolling through microfilm of The South London Press from June 1947 at the Wandsworth Heritage Service, searching for something else, when the headline about Miss Lancaster caught my eye. The few short paragraphs of the accompanying article conveyed a vivid impression of this unfazable and entrepreneurial woman.

KNITTING FOR SPAIN IN THE PEOPLE'S BOOKSHOP

In 1936 civil war broke out in Spain when Franco's fascists attempted to overthrow the democratically elected Popular Front government (also known as Republicans). In Britain, as in many other countries, there was widespread support on the Left and amongst working class people for the embattled Republican fighters. Activists in Battersea organised an 'Aid to Spain' week in December.

ON THE MARRIAGE OF CATHERINE BOUCHER TO WILLIAM BLAKE

The oldest church in Battersea is St Mary's, situated right next to the river. One if its claims to fame is that it was here that William Blake got married. The register shows he married Catherine Boucher, a young woman who grew up in what was then the small village of Battersea. Catherine marked the register with an X, as she was illiterate, which I found very poignant. After they were married William taught her to read and write. Catherine was more than a muse to Blake, taking charge of their finances and working alongside him at the printing press. She must have been quite a strong character to take on someone like William Blake.

WHAT'S MRS DESPARD EVER DONE FOR US

Nine Elms in Battersea was a notorious slum in the late 19th and early 20th century. In 1890, a wealthy widow, Charlotte Despard, moved to the area to bring relief to the poor and try to improve conditions. From our 21st century viewpoint, you might assume that she was a do-gooder and that the locals probably found her patronising. However, a talk by the historian Penelope Corfield at Battersea Arts Centre inspired me to research Charlotte Despard. The two available biographies reveal that she was a progressive and radical woman, and that in fact her neighbours loved and venerated her. She was also involved in the suffragette movement and was one of the first women to stand for Parliament in the 1918 general election. Unfortunately, she lost.

BATTERSEA WOMEN'S PUB OUTING

In my local pub, the Mason's Arms, there's a wonderful black and white photo of a group of women standing in front of, and hanging out of, a bus, either on their way to or just returned from their annual seaside outing. The handwritten inscription reads 'Mason's Arms Women's Outing June 16th 1947'. I've not been able to track down any more detail about the photo. The photographer Grace Robertson took photos of similar pub outings in the 1950s.

Visit the London Undercurrents blog for more background information londonundercurrents.wordpress.com

ACKNOWLEDGEMENTS

Gratitude to the editors of the following publications, where
several of our poems first appeared, sometimes in different
versions:

*South Bank Poetry, Brittle Star, Lunar Poetry, Severine, Well
Versed, Ink Sweat & Tears, Battersea Matters* and *The Pocket
Poetry Book of Suffrage* from Paper Swans Press.

A big shout out to all the libraries, websites, and authors, too
numerous to mention here, who made it possible for us to
uncover, research and write about the real and
imagined women in our local areas of London. Special thanks
to London Metropolitan Archives, Wandsworth Heritage
Service, Wandsworth Libraries, Islington Libraries and
council website.

The full bibliography and details of further reading and
research materials can be found on our blog:
https://londonundercurrents.wordpress.com/bibliography

Thanks for support and encouragement of our project,
especially in the early days, goes to Agnes Meadows, Sue
Johns, Jacqueline Gabbitas, Martin Parker, Peter Ebsworth,
Katherine Lockton, Hylda Sims, Caroline Vero, Angela
Brodie, Peter Raynard, and Camilla Reeve. For believing in
our book thank you to Abegail Morley, Against the Grain
Press and for vocal support thank you Paper Swans Press.

For awarding us Research and Development funding, thank you
to Arts Council England, and to Laura Kenwright at Spread the
Word, Catherine Rogers and Gemma Seltzer for help in
navigating the funding application process. For providing a
place for us to write and explore, thank you Spread the Word.

151

An extra special Thank You goes to the brilliant Jacqueline Saphra whose mentorship pushed us to be better poets, and more rounded people.

Last, but definitely not least, a big Thank You to all the women of London, past, present and future. May you shine.

Joolz and Hilaire

Holland Park Press is a unique publishing initiative. Its aim is to promote poetry and literary fiction, and discover new writers. It specialises in contemporary English fiction and poetry, and translations of Dutch classics. It also gives contemporary Dutch writers the opportunity to be published in Dutch and English.

To

Learn more about Joolz and Hilaire
Discover other interesting books
Read our unique Anglo-Dutch magazine
Find out how to submit your manuscript
Take part in one of our competitions

Visit www.hollandparkpress.co.uk

Bookshop: http://www.hollandparkpress.co.uk/books.php

Holland Park Press in the social media:

http://www.twitter.com/HollandParkPres
http://www.facebook.com/HollandParkPress
http://www.linkedin.com/company/holland-park-press
http://www.youtube.com/user/HollandParkPress
http://plus.google.com/+HollandParkPress